AF885286

MIND ON MY MONEY

WORKBOOK

PLAN. POCKET. PROTECT.

DR. RAYKEL TOLSON

Paperback ISBN: 978-1-7347932-7-7

Published and distributed by Tolson Publishing

Dear Reader,

Thank you for purchasing the "Mind On My Money Workbook: Plan. Pocket. Protect." I am deeply grateful for your investment in this transformative journey toward financial freedom.

My desire to close the wealth gap in America, particularly the racial gap and the divide between the top 10 percent and the rest of Americans, has driven me to create this workbook. It is my mission to empower individuals like you with the knowledge and tools to build generational wealth, ensuring that financial prosperity is within everyone's reach.

Your decision to invest in your financial education is a powerful step toward securing a brighter future. By cultivating an abundance mindset, mastering budgeting, and protecting your wealth, you are paving the way for financial freedom not only for yourself but for your children and their children. Your commitment to this journey will undoubtedly bless your future self and generations to come.

Thank you once again for choosing "Mind On My Money Workbook." Together, we can reduce the wealth gap one family at a time.

Blessings,

Dr. Raykel Tolson

www.raykeltolson.com

Let the Lord be magnified, which hath pleasure in the prosperity of his servant. - Psalm 35:27

To create wealth that will provide financial freedom for generations, **you must get your mind on your money.** To build generational wealth and achieve financial freedom, you need to think about your money in a way that goes beyond the typical mindset. Like the complaints; I have to pay bills, the gas prices are too high, or you have robbed Peter to pay Paul. Cultivate a healthy money mindset before you get your mind on your money. Cultivating a healthy money mindset involves adopting certain attitudes, habits, and practices that align with financial success. The most important thing you must do is to believe that **God is a ceaseless flow of substance**. Remember that God will supply every need of yours according to his riches in glory in Christ Jesus (Philippians 4:19). Adopt an abundance mindset, believing that there are ample opportunities for wealth creation. I have included affirmations to help elevate your money mindset.

Get your mind on ABUNDANCE!

- **Recognize Scarcity Mentality**: Understand that scarcity mentality entails believing that there are limited resources, opportunities, and success. These beliefs lead to fear, competition, and a sense of lack. Acknowledge if thoughts of lack and scarcity plague you, and consciously choose to shift your mindset towards abundance.
- **Reframe Challenges as Opportunities**: Embrace challenges and setbacks as opportunities for growth and learning. Instead of viewing obstacles as roadblocks, reframe them as stepping stones to progress. Look for the lessons and possibilities that come with each challenge, and maintain a positive perspective on how they can contribute to your personal and professional development.

Developing an abundance mindset is an ongoing practice that requires conscious effort and consistent reinforcement. Be patient with yourself and commit to nurturing an abundant perspective in all aspects of your life. Over time, you will see the positive shifts and the opportunities that come from embracing abundance.

- **Celebrate Others' Success**: Avoid comparing yourself to others and feeling envious or resentful of their success. Instead, celebrate their achievements and see them as evidence that success is attainable and abundant. Embrace a mindset of collaboration and abundance, recognizing that there is enough success and prosperity for everyone.
- **Focus on Abundance in All Areas of Life**: Expand your mindset beyond just financial abundance. Recognize the abundance in relationships, health, opportunities, and personal growth. Emphasize the abundance of love, joy, knowledge, and experiences that surround you daily. By recognizing abundance in all aspects of life, you shift your overall perspective towards a mindset of abundance.
- **Practice Visualization and Affirmations**: Engage in visualization exercises where you imagine yourself already living in a state of abundance. Visualize the life you desire, envisioning the success, prosperity, and fulfillment you want to achieve. Use positive affirmations that reinforce abundance and prosperity, repeating empowering statements such as "I attract abundance into my life" or "I am worthy of wealth and success."
- **Take Inspired Action:** Action must accompany an abundance mindset. Set goals, create action plans, and take consistent steps towards your desired outcomes. By taking inspired action, you align yourself with the opportunities and possibilities that abundance offers. Purchasing this workbook was a great start.

What will you do to create an abundance mindset?

Affirmations To Develop An Abundance Mindset

I am worthy of abundance in all areas of my life.

Prosperity flows to me **effortlessly and continuously.**

I attract wealth and success with ease.

I speak words that are aligned with **abundance** and gratitude.

I know that there is unlimited wealth.

I feel more financially **secure.**

I am a magnet for financial prosperity.

I attract opportunities for growth and abundance everywhere.

My actions create constant wealth, prosperity, and abundance.

I am grateful for the **abundance** that I have and the abundance on its way.

I know **I deserve** to live a life of **financial freedom** and security.

I love that **money flows freely** and easily to me.

I see new and exciting ways **to receive income.**

Abundance is my **natural state of being**.

I am **constantly attracting** opportunities that create more money.

Exercise: Create your own affirmations.

Get your mind on FORGIVENESS!

In the journey towards financial abundance, one often overlooked but crucial step is forgiveness. Holding onto resentment, guilt, or anger can create mental and emotional blocks that hinder your progress and keep you from achieving the financial freedom you desire. Forgiveness can clear these blocks and open up pathways to abundance.

Forgiveness of God

For many, financial struggles can lead to questioning their faith or feeling abandoned by a higher power. It's important to reconcile these feelings and forgive any perceived grievances with God. Understanding that challenges are often opportunities for growth and that **God wants you to prosper** can be liberating. Embrace the idea that abundance is a divine right and trust the process.

Exercise: Reflect on your spiritual beliefs and write any feelings of resentment or doubt you may have. Then write a prayer or affirmation that helps you release these feelings and affirm your trust in divine abundance.

Forgiveness of Parents

Our financial habits and beliefs are often inherited from our parents. Sometimes, parents pass down misinformation or fail to teach essential financial skills. Forgive your parents for any financial misguidance, recognizing that they did the best they could with the knowledge they had. Use this understanding to break the cycle and create a healthier financial future for yourself.

Exercise: Write any financial advice or beliefs inherited from your parents that you feel were unhelpful. Then, write a note of forgiveness to them, understanding that they were influenced by their circumstances.

Forgiveness of Self

We all make mistakes, especially with our money. Whether it's debt, poor investments, or simply not saving enough, it's easy to be harsh on ourselves. However, self-forgiveness is essential to move forward. **Accept your past mistakes, learn from them, and let them go**. This will free you from guilt and enable you to make better financial decisions.

Exercise: Write a letter to yourself forgiving any past financial mistakes. Highlight what you've learned and how these experiences have made you wiser.

Forgiveness of Those Who Have Harmed You Financially

Financial harm from others, whether through fraud, deceit, or unpaid debts, can leave deep scars. Holding onto these grievances can prevent you from trusting others. When you forgive those who have done you harm does not mean you are condoning their actions. It means releasing the emotional burden they've caused. **This release is crucial for your financial healing and progress.**

Exercise: List individuals who have harmed you financially and describe how their actions affected you. Then, write a note of forgiveness, focusing on freeing yourself from the negative emotions tied to these experiences.

Moving Forward with Forgiveness

Forgiveness is not about forgetting or excusing wrongdoings. It's about releasing the emotional hold these experiences have on you. By forgiving God, yourself, society, your parents, and those who have harmed you financially, you open yourself up to new opportunities and the flow of abundance.

Remember, abundance is as much a state of mind as it is a state of being. By practicing forgiveness, you clear the path for prosperity to enter your life and set the stage for a healthier, wealthier future.

Exercise: Spend a few moments each day practicing forgiveness through meditation or journaling. Visualize the release of negative emotions and the influx of positive, abundant energy. This practice will reinforce your commitment to an abundant mindset and financial success.

Forgiveness Mantra

I forgive, release it, and am grateful for the lesson learned.

I know that all is working for my good.

Get your mind on GRATITUDE!

Gratitude is one of the most powerful tools you can cultivate to attract and maintain abundance. When you adopt an attitude of gratitude, you **shift your focus from what you lack to what you have**, opening the door to greater prosperity and fulfillment. Think about it: how can you attract more of what you desire if you're constantly focused on what you lack? Gratitude unlocks the door to abundance by shifting your mindset from scarcity to appreciation. It's the **Secret Weapon** that fuels your financial journey.

Enhancing Financial Awareness

Being grateful for what you have encourages you to take better care of your finances. Appreciating your income, savings, and investments, you're more likely to make thoughtful and informed financial decisions. **Gratitude fosters a sense of responsibility and stewardship**, motivating you to manage your resources wisely.

Exercise: Reflect on your financial achievements and milestones. List them out and express gratitude for each one, acknowledging the effort and discipline that made them possible.

The Power of Positive Focus

Gratitude changes your perspective. Instead of dwelling on financial challenges and shortcomings, a gratitude mindset helps you appreciate your current resources and opportunities. This positive focus can reduce stress, increase motivation, and foster a sense of contentment. When you feel good about your financial situation, you're more likely to make decisions that lead to further prosperity.

Exercise: Start a gratitude journal. Each day, write three things you are grateful for in your financial life, no matter how small. This practice will help you maintain a positive focus and attract more abundance.

Strengthening Relationships

Gratitude extends beyond your personal finances and into your relationships. Appreciating the support and contributions of others can strengthen your professional network and personal connections. Be grateful for the people in your life. Have you heard of **Six Degrees of Kevin Bacon**? It is a famous social experiment highlighting the small world phenomenon and the interconnectedness of individuals within the entertainment industry. It illustrates the notion that we are connected to one another through a surprisingly small number of steps or associations, emphasizing the idea of a closely interconnected world. **Be grateful for all your associations because they know someone who might provide the resources you need.**

Exercise: Create a list of people who have positively impacted your financial journey. Whether it's a mentor, a family member, or a colleague, expressing your gratitude can deepen your relationships and open doors to future opportunities. Send a thank you note or call to thank them.

Attracting More Abundance

The law of attraction suggests that like attracts like. When you express gratitude for the financial blessings you have, you create a positive energy that attracts more of the same. This doesn't mean ignoring financial difficulties; rather, it's about finding something to be thankful for in every situation. This mindset can lead to new opportunities and unexpected sources of income.

When faced with a financial challenge, look for a silver lining. Write one positive aspect or lesson from the situation and express gratitude for it. This practice will help you maintain a positive outlook, even during tough times.

Embrace Gratitude for Financial Abundance

Gratitude is more than just a feel-good emotion; it's a powerful practice that can transform your financial life. Be grateful for all the resources you have. When we think of resources, we often think of money and things. However, **your greatest resource is YOU**! Be grateful for you, your creativity, knowledge, wisdom, courage, resilience, passion, drive, and your desire to be the best version of YOU. Make gratitude a daily habit and watch as your financial situation improves and your sense of fulfillment grows.

Exercise: Set aside a few minutes each day to meditate on gratitude. Close your eyes, take deep breaths, and mentally list everything you are grateful for in your financial life. This simple practice can reinforce your gratitude mindset and help you attract more abundance.

Purchase my I AM Blessed Journal to begine your gratitude practice on Amazon.

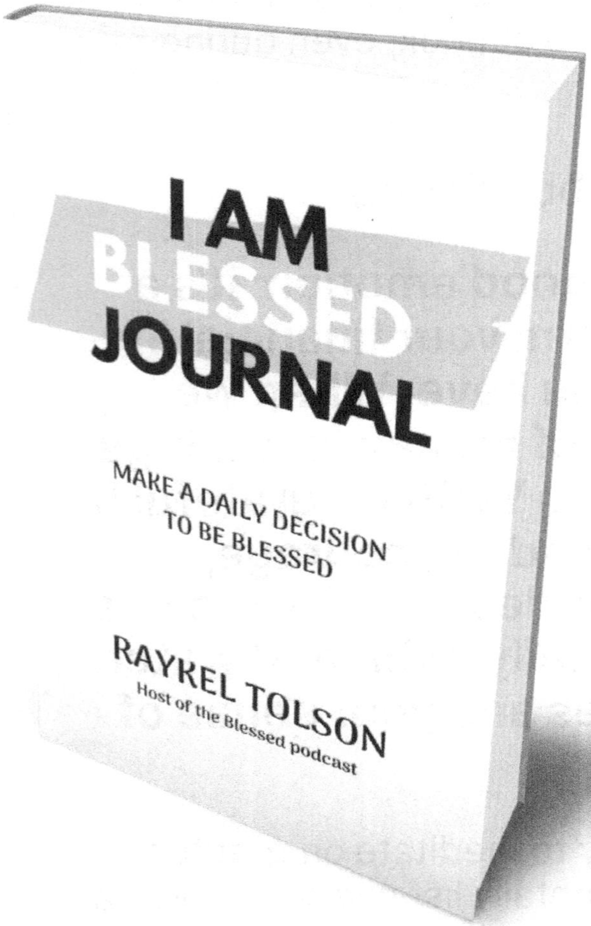

The “I Am Blessed Journal” is your companion for a spiritually enriching journey, designed to elevate your thoughts and attract positivity into your life. Each week, you'll find empowering affirmations called Thought Elevations, along with dedicated space to record your daily blessings and the lessons you've learned. This journal also includes space to write a weekly prayer of gratitude, encouraging you to cultivate a heart of thankfulnes.s

SCAN ME

PLAN INTENTIONALLY

"Good planning and hard work lead to prosperity." - Proverbs 21:5 (NLT)

Many people don't have a plan for their finances. We have very general dreams like, "One day, I'd like to pay for my kid's college education. One day, I'd like to retire." Creating a plan is necessary to accomplish any goal.

Before you can make financial plans, it is **essential to know where you are currently**. Can you answer the question, **what is your net worth?** Do you know how much money you have in your savings and checking account? How much you have in a company IRA? How much equity you currently have in your home? Last one, do you know how much your car is worth? These are a few things required to determine your net worth. Don't feel bad if you don't know the answer to these questions because many people are unaware. Nevertheless, it is an excellent place to start in determining your financial goals.

Get your mind on your BUDGET!

Knowing your current spending habits is another vital fact to gather before making financial plans. It is unrealistic to think you will save $300 when you only have $150 remaining after your expenses. Most people hate the word **BUDGET** because they feel like it is restrictive. However, it would help if you thought of a budget as a way to **be intentional in your spending**. Setting a budget or spending plan ensures you direct your money to your **financial priorities,** and not all to Starbucks, Amazon, or Target. (These places used to get too much of my money.)

Before we discuss how to budget, let's find out where your money is currently going. This will help you determine what your spending priorities are currently.

Budgeting Exercise: Tracking Your Spending for One Month

Set Up Your Log:

- Choose a method for tracking your expenses: a physical notebook, a spreadsheet, a budgeting app, or by paying for everything with your debit or credit card.
- If using a notebook or spreadsheet, create columns for the date, description of the expense, category (e.g., groceries, entertainment, utilities), and amount spent.

Commit to Tracking Every Expense:

- For the next 30 days, commit to logging every single purchase you make, no matter how small.
- If you choose to use a debit or credit card for all transactions, it will simplify the tracking process, as you can refer to your bank or credit card statements.

Categorize Your Spending:

- As you log each expense, categorize it into predefined categories such as groceries, dining out, transportation, entertainment, bills, etc.
- This will help you see patterns in your spending habits.

Review and Reflect Weekly:

- At the end of each week, review your expenses to ensure you've logged everything accurately.
- Reflect on your spending patterns and consider areas where you may cut back or make adjustments.

End of Month Analysis:

- At the end of the month, total up your expenses in each category.
- Analyze where most of your money is going and identify any surprising areas where you may be overspending.
- Consider whether your spending aligns with your financial goals and values.

There are several budgeting plans or methods that individuals can use to manage their finances effectively. Here are explanations of some popular budgeting plans:

- **50/30/20 Budgeting:** The 50/30/20 budgeting rule suggests allocating 50% of your income to needs (essential expenses like housing, utilities, and groceries), 30% to wants (discretionary expenses like entertainment and dining out), and 20% to savings and debt repayment.
- **80/20 Budgeting**: The 80/20 budgeting method involves allocating 80% of your income to expenses, savings, and debt repayment while reserving 20% for long-term savings, investments, or other financial goals.
- **Envelope Budgeting**: With envelope budgeting, you assign specific amounts of cash to different categories or envelopes representing different spending categories (e.g., groceries, transportation). You can only spend the cash allocated in each envelope, helping you control your spending and stay within budget.
- **Value-Based Budgeting:** With value-based budgeting, you align your spending with your personal values and priorities. You identify your core values and allocate your income towards expenses that reflect those values. This approach helps ensure that your spending aligns with what matters most to you.

The Importance of Giving 10 Percent to Church or Charity When Budgeting

Incorporating the practice of **giving 10 percent** of your income to your church or a chosen charity into your budget is not only a demonstration of generosity, but also a powerful act of financial stewardship. This principle, often referred to as tithing, encourages a mindset of abundance and gratitude, reinforcing the belief that there is always enough to share. By consistently allocating a portion of your earnings to support others, you foster a sense of community and purpose, contribute to meaningful causes, and invite positive financial energy into your life. Additionally, this habit will instill discipline and a sense of priority in your financial planning, **ensuring that your money management aligns with your values and spiritual beliefs.**

Prepare Your Budget

It's important to choose a budgeting plan that aligns with your financial goals, lifestyle, and personal preferences. You may also combine elements of different budgeting plans to create a customized budgeting approach that works best for you. **Regularly reviewing and adjusting your budget** as needed is key to staying on track and maintaining financial control.

Be kind with yourself while you are creating new spending and savings habits. Use the budget worksheet on the next page to help you get on track. Also, reassess your plan once a year to ensure you stay on track. It's like seeing your doctor once a year for a checkup. If you do this, it prevents any major issues from coming up.

Exercise: Create your budget on the next page.

Budget

Monthly Income ______________________

Expenses	Budgeted Amount	Actually Spent
Mortgage/Rent		
Electric		
Gas		
Water		
Waste Disposal		
Groceries		
Internet		
Phone		
Auto		
Auto Expenses		
Car Insurance		
Health Insurances (medical, dental, vision)		
Renter's Insurance		
Life Insurance		
Personal Care(Grooming & Clothing)		
Tithes/Charity		
Savings		
Dining Out/Coffee		
Entertainment		

Budget continued

Expense	Budgeted Amount	Actually Spent

Debt	Interest Rate	Credit Limit	Current Balance	Monthly Payment

My Net Worth Worksheet

What I Own	Value	What I Owe	Net Value
ex. house car 401k IUL	400,000 20,000 30,000 10,000	300,000 13,000	100,000 7,000 30,000 10,000

Buying things that hold value or grow in value is key!

Worksheet 2

What I Own	Value	What I Owe	Net Value

Get your mind on SAVING!

In the journey toward financial stability and prosperity, saving money is a foundational practice that cannot be overstated. **Saving plays a crucial role in ensuring your financial well-being**. The more you save, the closer you get to financial independence. A healthy savings account empowers you to make choices based on your values and goals, not just your paycheck.

I can hear some of you saying, "But I don't have enough money to save." I understand, but you can find hidden cash once you know what you spend monthly. My company calls it the **Find the Money Funnel**. You may need to refinance your finances. Maybe you are paying too much for services and subscriptions.

Finding Balance in Your Finances

The best place to find hidden money is in your spending. Buying a coffee pot and a To-Go coffee cup will save you money for high-priced coffee drinks. And if you're lucky, your employer has invested in a Keurig, so all you need is the coffee pod and cup.

I'm not suggesting that you should stop all trips to coffee shops, movie theaters, restaurants, or anything else you enjoy. **Enjoying life's little pleasures is important for your overall well-being and happiness.** However, it's crucial to strike a balance between spending on these enjoyable activities and ensuring you are saving money for your future. **By being mindful of your spending and not splurging excessively, you can still indulge in your favorite activities while steadily building a secure financial foundation.**

Prioritize Your Spending

Prioritizing your spending is essential for achieving financial stability and reaching your long-term goals. By identifying and focusing on what truly matters, you can ensure that your money is being used effectively. Maybe going on a weekly date with your significant other or subscribing to the Disney Channel for movie night with your children is equally important as paying your mortgage. That is perfectly fine. That just means that you can cut spending elsewhere. This approach helps you avoid unnecessary expenditures, reduce financial stress, and make informed decisions that align with your values and aspirations. **By prioritizing your spending, you take control of your finances, paving the way for a more secure and prosperous future.**

Consider this:

Saving $150 monthly, you will have $1800 at the end of the year for a nice vacation instead of putting it on a credit card.

Investing that $150 every month at 8% interest over 20 years, you will have $85,350 for retirement.

What are your financial goals?

A few financial goals to consider:

- **Emergency Fund** - The primary purpose of an emergency fund is to cover unforeseen financial emergencies or unexpected expenses. These could include medical emergencies, car repairs, home repairs, job loss, or any other urgent expenses that you did not expect. An emergency fund provides a sense of financial security and peace of mind. It helps you cope with the financial impact of emergencies without causing significant disruption to your overall financial well-being. It's crucial to keep the emergency fund in a highly liquid and easily accessible account. **Financial experts generally recommend having three to six months' worth of living expense**s saved in your emergency fund.
- **Kids College Fund** - Set a savings goal based on the estimated future college costs. **Consider how much you want to contribute toward your child's education and how much you expect them to contribute through scholarships, grants, work-study programs, or their own savings.** The amount you need to save will be influenced by the time remaining until your child enters college. The earlier you save, the more time your investments have to grow and potentially offset future costs. It's essential to consider inflation rates when estimating future college expenses and adjust your savings goal accordingly.
- **Home Fund** -Traditionally, a down payment of **20% of the home's purchase price recommended to avoid private mortgage insurance (PMI)**. However, it's important to note that many lenders now offer loan options with lower down payment requirements. For example, some conventional loans may require a down payment of as low as 5% of the purchase price, while **FHA loans can have down payments as low as 3.5%**. In addition to the down payment, add the **closing costs, which typically range from 2% to 5% of the purchase price**. These costs cover expenses such as loan origination fees, appraisal fees, title insurance, and attorney fees.

Exercise: Write your financial goals

Bonus: Why do you want the goal?

Goal	Why I Want It	$ Needed	$ Saved

Continue Goals

Goal	Why I Want It	$ Needed	$ Saved

Get your mind on a SIDE HUSTLE!

If you don't earn enough money to cover your expenses and save, then you need to discover a way to increase your income. You could get a different W-2 job that pays more or get a part-time W-2 job. Or you can join the millions of people who have a side hustle. **A side hustle, or secondary job, provides a valuable opportunity to diversify your income streams, achieve your financial goals more rapidly, and enhance your financial security**. Relying on a single income can be precarious, especially in an unstable job market. A side hustle or secondary job acts as a safety net, offering an additional stream of income that can help cover unexpected expenses, pay down debt, or contribute to savings. An extra financial cushion can reduce stress and provide peace of mind, knowing you have a backup plan if your primary income source is disrupted.

The Importance of a Side Hustle

I rarely suggest that people get a part time W-2 job unless it provides exceptional perks that are important to you, like free flights or free hotel rooms. I'm so grateful that my son kept his part-time job at Delta Airlines, because those flight benefits are everything. I suggest everyone has a side hustle, even those W-2 professionals who have enough money to save. Having a side hustle not only provides additional income but also **offers several tax advantages**. Expenses related to your side hustle, such as supplies, equipment, home office expenses, and even mileage, can often be deducted from your taxable income. You may also qualify for special deductions and credits available to self-employed individuals, such as the Qualified Business Income Deduction (QBI) and the Home Office Deduction. Keeping meticulous records of your income and expenses is crucial to maximizing these tax benefits, ultimately reducing your overall tax liability and potentially increasing your net earnings from your side hustle. Always consult with a tax professional to ensure you're taking full advantage of all available deductions and credits related to your specific side hustle activities.

Embrace the Side Hustle

Engaging in a side hustle allows you to explore interests and develop skills outside of your primary job. This can lead to **personal growth**, increased job satisfaction, and even new career opportunities. Whether it's freelancing, starting a small business, or offering services in a field you're passionate about, a side hustle can provide a creative outlet and a chance to pursue your passions.

Here are just a few ideas for a side hustles:

- Network Marketing
- Affiliate Marketing
- Dropshipping
- Rideshare Driver
- Sell Digital Products
- Freelancer
- Coach/Consultant
- Deliver Groceries/Food
- Rent Your Home/Room
- Teach people to Plan Intentionally, Pocket Wisely & Protect Fiercely (**Contact me at www.raykeltolson.com if you would like to learn more about helping your community Protect Their Coins and creating millionaires without a ball or microphone.**)

Exercise: List your skills, hobbies, and interests that could potentially be monetized. Research side hustle opportunities. Identify one potential side hustle idea that excites you. Create a simple action plan outlining the steps you need to take to get started, and commit to dedicating a specific amount of time each week to developing your side hustle.

The Widow's Olive Oil

The wife of a man from the company of the prophets cried out to Elisha, "Your servant my husband is dead, and you know that he revered the Lord. **But now his creditor is coming** to take my two boys as his slaves."

Elisha replied to her, "How can I help you? **Tell me, what do you have in your house?"**

"Your servant has nothing there at all," she said, "except a small jar of olive oil."

Elisha said, "**Go around and ask all your neighbors for empty jars. Don't ask for just a few**. Then go inside and shut the door behind you and your sons. Pour oil into all the jars, and as each is filled, put it to one side."

She left him and shut the door behind her and her sons. They brought the jars to her and she kept pouring. When all the jars were full, she said to her son, "Bring me another one."

But he replied, "There is not a jar left." Then the oil stopped flowing.

She went and told the man of God, and he said, "**Go, sell the oil and pay your debts. You and your sons can live on what is left**."

What do you have in your house?

Like the widow in the story above, you need to use what you already have and allow God to bless it.

Gifts/Talents/Skills/Hobbies/Interests	Possible Side Hustle

Continue

Gifts/Talents/Skills/Hobbies/Interests	Possible Side Hustle

POCKET WISELY

"But divide your investments among many places, for you do not know what risks might lie ahead. " - Ecclesiastes 11:2 (NLT)

Get your mind on the RULE OF 72!

One of the most powerful aspects of saving is the potential for compound growth. When deciding where to pocket your money, you must understand the **Rule of 72**. The Rule of 72 is a simplified mathematical rule that provides an estimate of how long it will take for an investment or debt to double in value or size, respectively, based on a fixed interest rate. It is a useful tool for quickly estimating the impact of compounding on investments or the growth of debt.

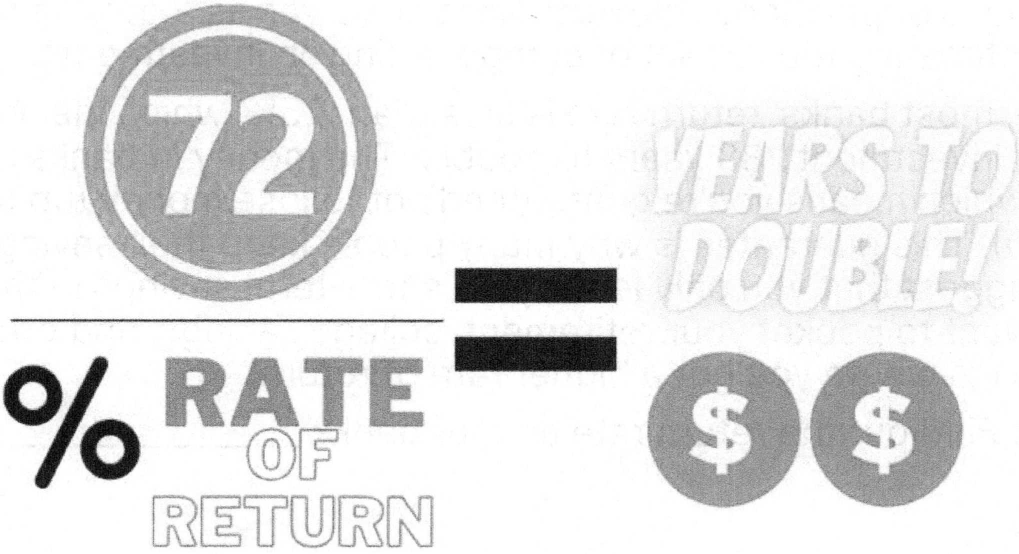

SCAN ME

“

“Compound interest is the eighth wonder of the world. He who understands it, earns it ...

Here's how it works:

If you want to estimate how long it will take for an investment to double in value, divide 72 by the annual interest rate or rate of return you expect to earn on that investment. The result will be the approximate number of years it will take for the investment to double. For example, if you expect an investment to earn a 6% annual return, using the Rule of 72, you can estimate that it will take approximately 12 years (72 / 6 = 12) for the investment to double in value.

It's important to note that the Rule of 72 provides an approximation and assumes a fixed interest rate. It does not account for factors such as compounding frequency, fluctuating interest rates, or additional contributions or payments. Nevertheless, it serves as a quick and easy tool for estimating the impact of compounding on investments.

Currently, most banks' return rate is less than .25%, which means it will take your investment 288 years to double. The money in banks is FDIC insured, which means you're guaranteed not to lose money (up to $250,000). This guarantee is why many people keep their savings in the bank. I suggest that you only leave your short-term savings in the bank. You will want to pocket your retirement, college savings, and other long term savings where you get a higher rate of return.

Exercise: Find out the return rate at your bank? ____________________

Get your mind on TAXES!

We can only talk about pocketing money if we discuss taxes. The fundamental difference between the rich and the middle class is the amount paid in taxes. Rich people spend a lot of money on tax accountants and advisors to lower their tax bills. They are also business owners and not employees. Study the picture below to learn how the different vehicles used to invest your money will determine when your obligations to Uncle Sam occur.

Exercise: Scan the QR code and watch the video about the impact of taxes. Then determine your tax bracket.

SCAN ME

Get your mind on RETIREMENT!

Here is why you need to get your mind on your retirement:

- 30% of retirees rely on Social Security as their sole source of income.
- The average monthly Social Security benefit for retired workers is $1,681 and is set to rise to only $1,827 in 2023.
- 55% of Americans say they're behind on saving for retirement
- 38% of Americans are worried about outliving their savings and investments
- 44% of retirees struggle to afford basic living expenses.

(https://listwithclever.com/research/retirement-finances-2023/)

Retirement Planning

When it comes to retirement planning, most people wait until they are in their 50s. Waiting this long to create a retirement plan means you will need to work longer or forgo the dreams of traveling and sitting on the beach reading romance novels. We may have different goals for retirement, but all of us **desire the FREEDOM to do whatever we want to do wherever we choose to do it.**

Scan QR code to watch video about retirement planning.

SCAN ME

Your retirement may seem far off, but it's closer than you think. And the average American will spend at least 20 years in retirement. And for non-smokers in excellent health, there is a one in three chance women will live to age 95 or beyond and a one in five chance men will live to age 95 or beyond. Therefore, you may need enough money to live for 30 years in retirement. The earlier you can start retirement savings, the more money you accumulate, and the less likely you will run out of money.

When planning for retirement, these should be your first steps:

1. **Get your Social Security Statement** to review the estimates of your future retirement, disability, and survivors' benefits. Go to www.ssa.gov to get your free and secure my Social Security account where you can estimate your future benefits.

2. **Learn about retirement savings plans through your employer**. Many employers will match an employee's contributions in a 401(k). That is free money you don't want to miss out on.

3. **Open your own retirement account**. I suggest you look into both a Roth IRA and an indexed universal life (IUL) policy. Contact me for more information at www.raykeltolson.com on these options.

4. **Start saving for retirement NOW!** The earlier the better, but later is better than never!

5. Scan the QR code to **Watch our FREE virtual Money 101 workshop**

Exercise: Watch Money 101 webinar and take notes

Exercise: Compute how much you currently have for retirement. Then determine what you will need to retire comfortably?

RETIREMENT WORKSHEET

This retirement worksheet serves as a planning tool to help you estimate your future financial needs and identify any potential gaps between your retirement income and expenses.

EXPECTED MONTHLY INCOME

Social Security Benefits ____________________

Pension ____________________

401k ____________________

IRA ____________________

IUL ____________________

Annuity ____________________

Rental Income ____________________

Other Passive Income ____________________

EXPECTED MONTHLY EXPENSES

Mortgage/Rent ________ Groceries ________

Real Estate Taxes ________ Dining Out ________

Property Insurance ______ Grooming ________

Entertainment __________ Utilities __________

Internet/Cable _______ Phone __________

Health Insurance ________ Auto ____________

Prescriptions ____________ Travel ___________

Auto Insurance ________ Tithes/Charity_______

Auto Expenses __________ Personal____________

I added property taxes and insurance for those who will have paid off their homes. Many people forget these expenses still need to be paid.

If you want **to retire with 1 million dollars at age 65**.

Start at **age 25**, you will need to save **$325 per month at a rate of 8%.**

Start at **age 35**, you will need to save **$750 per month at a rate of 8%.**

Start at **age 45**, you will need to save **$1800 per month at a rate of 8%.**

Don't panic if you're **50** and haven't started saving for retirement yet. **You can reach $1 million if you adjust your retirement age to 70** and save $1800 per month at a rate of 8%. If you are older than 50, then you will need to invest much more.

Retiring with 1 million dollars will provide roughly $75,000 annually. You might only need a retirement income of $35,000 annually when added to your other sources, which means you don't need 1 million dollars.

Get your mind on LEAVING AN INHERITANCE!

"

Good people leave an inheritance to their grandchildren. - Proverbs 13:22

Based on the Rule of 72, it will take less money to leave **$1 million dollars for your newborn**. Saving **only $150 per month** for 50 years at a rate of 8% would give your child $1,000,000. Wouldn't you be happy to have your parents call to tell you there will be or is $1 million dollars waiting for you when you turn 50?

Leaving a Legacy

While writing this workbook, many people around the United States are angry that Lebron James's son, Bronny, was just drafted by the Los Angeles Lakers after only one year playing college basketball. And many don't feel the young man is good enough to play in the NBA yet. There is an uproar that Lebron helped his son get the job.

I applaud Lebron for opening doors for his son. My son got his job at Delta Airlines because my friend recommended him. In fact, my motivation to purchase my duplex in Los Angeles was to provide a home for my son when he graduated from college. And if I can do anything else legally to help my son, you better believe that I will.

Percy Miller, aka Master P, launched his career and subsequent business empire using the proceeds from a life insurance policy left by his grandfather. This initial capital was pivotal in starting No Limit Records, which grew into a powerhouse in the 1990s, revolutionizing the hip-hop industry and beyond.

Master P's story underscores the power of financial planning and the lasting impact of generational foresight. It also proves that you don't have to be famous or a billionaire to open doors for your children and grandchildren. All you need to do is make a sound financial plan.

SCAN ME

Exercise: Scan the QR code to watch video then create a list of all the things you want to do for your children and grandchildren.

PROTECT FIERCELY

"A prudent person foresees danger and takes precautions. The simpleton goes blindly on and suffers the consequences."

-Proverbs 27:12 (NLT)

Get your mind on PROTECTING FROM MARKET RISKS!

Investing is a powerful tool for building wealth and achieving financial goals, but it comes with its share of uncertainties. One of the most significant factors you must contend with is market risks. Market risks refer to the potential for investment losses because factors that affect the entire market or a particular asset class. Investing in the stock market can produce higher rates of return, meaning your money doubles quicker. However, stock prices can be highly volatile, influenced by factors such as company performance, investor sentiment, economic indicators, and geopolitical events.

Managing Market Risks

While it is impossible to eliminate market risks entirely, investors can employ several strategies to manage and mitigate their impact. Diversification involves spreading investments across various asset classes, sectors, and geographical regions to reduce the impact of any single investment's poor performance. A well-diversified portfolio can help cushion against market volatility and provide more stable returns over time.

"

"But divide your investments among many places, for you do not know what risks might lie ahead. "-Ecclesiastes 11:2 (NLT)

The Bucket Strategy can be employed to reduce market risks, especially for your retirement and college savings that you don't want to lose. Scan the QR code and watch the explanation of the Bucket Strategy.

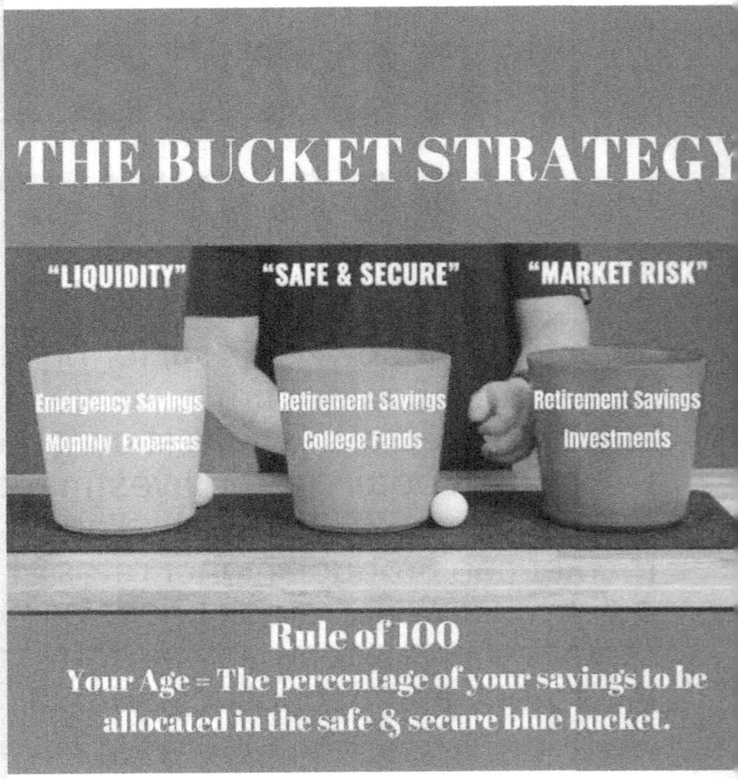

SCAN ME

Exercise: If you have money invested in the stock market (stocks, mutual funds, 401k), check to see the current rate of return. Also, check to see if the money has lost money.

Get your mind on LIFE INSURANCE!

A huge money mistake most people make is not having at all or enough insurance coverage. The Bible teaches in Proverbs 27:12, "**A prudent person foresees danger and takes precautions. The simpleton goes blindly on and suffers the consequences.**" Being underinsured most commonly happens with life insurance. No one likes talking about life insurance because it feels like you are preparing for death. Discussing life insurance involves confronting the topic of death, which can be uncomfortable and evoke feelings of fear or anxiety. Most People avoid these conversations because they prefer not to think about their mortality or that of their loved ones. And there is nothing fun about spending money on something you hope you'll never have to use.

Here are a few common negative beliefs people have about life insurance:

1. **It's a waste of money.** Some people erroneously believe that paying premiums for life insurance is a waste of money because they don't see an immediate return on investment. They think that if they don't die within the policy term, all the money spent on premiums is lost. However, the purpose of term is to replace your salary or pay off your mortgage if you die prematurely. Therefore, it is like purchasing car insurance, flood insurance, or any other insurance you get **just in case something bad happens.**
2. **It's too expensive.** Many individuals perceive life insurance as too expensive, especially when they are young and healthy. However, life insurance is cheaper when you are young and healthy.
3. **I don't need it.** Some individuals believe they don't need life insurance because they're young, healthy, single, or don't have dependents. They may underestimate the financial impact their death could have on their loved ones, such as covering funeral expenses, outstanding debts, or providing financial support.

Life Insurance = Love

If you lack adequate insurance, it can seriously upset your family's financial well-being. A life insurance policy's primary goal is to protect your loved ones if you die too soon. Purchasing a life insurance policy is a great way to show your family how much you love them.

There are thousands of Go Fund Me campaigns created each year to cover expenses life insurance would cover, such as funeral costs and other final expenses. However, it is good that families have this option when their loved ones refused to invest in a policy or was too old and unhealthy to afford a policy.

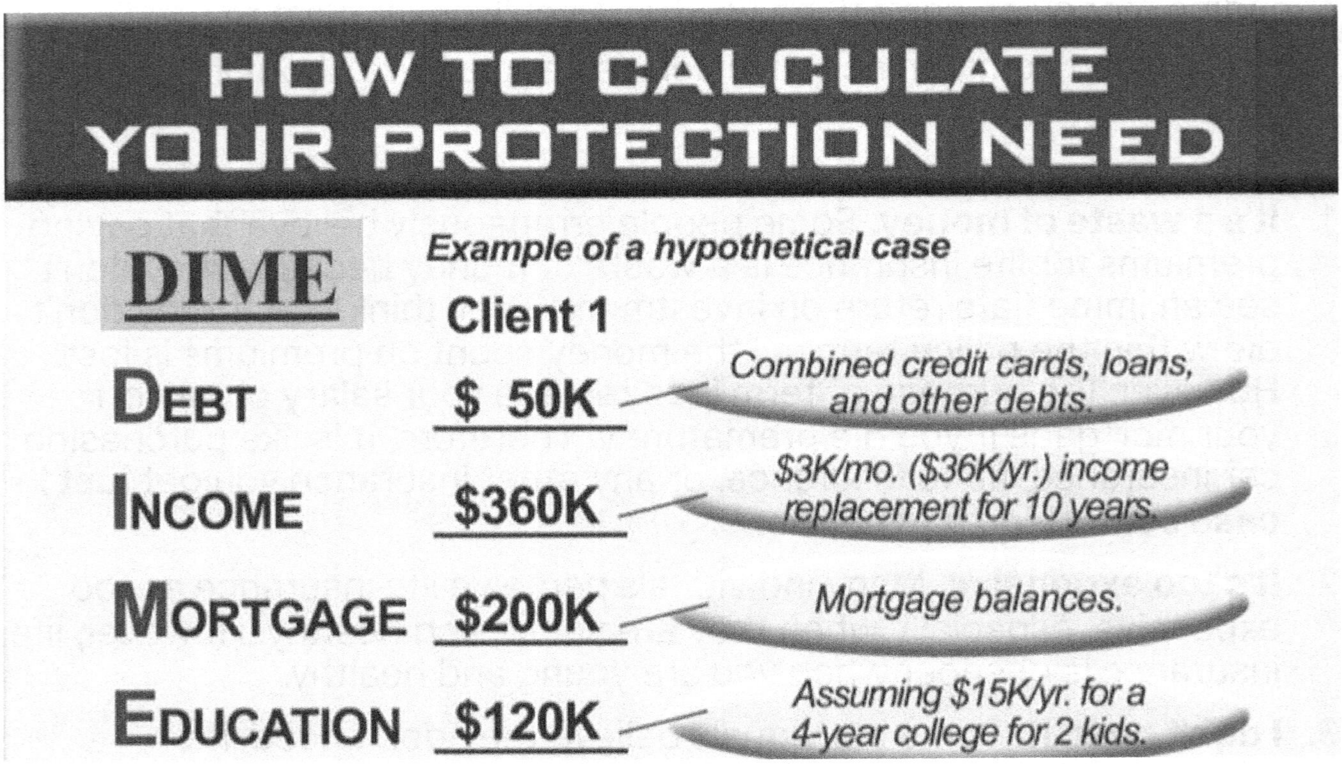

Exercise: Calculate how much life insurance you need to protect your family from having to create a Go Fund Me account or lose their home when you die.

DIME CALCULATION

DEBT ______________________

INCOME (10 years replacement) ______________________

MORTAGE (balance) ______________________

EDUCATION ______________________

AMOUNT INSURANCE NEEDED ______________________

Just in case you need a little more convincing why you should purchase life insurance, here are several common reasons you need to buy life insurance:

- **Financial Protection for Dependents:** Life insurance provides a financial safety net for your loved ones in the event of your untimely death. The death benefit can help replace lost income, cover daily living expenses, pay off debts, and fund future financial goals, such as education or retirement.
- **Debt Repayment:** Life insurance can ensure that any outstanding debts, such as a mortgage, personal loans, or credit card balances, are paid, preventing your loved ones from inheriting those financial obligations.
- **Funeral and Final Expenses:** Funerals and other end-of-life expenses can be costly. Life insurance can help cover these expenses, relieving the financial burden on your family during a difficult time.

- **Estate Planning**: Life insurance can be used as part of an estate planning strategy to preserve and transfer wealth to future generations. It can help provide liquidity to pay estate taxes, ensure fair distribution of assets, or create an inheritance for heirs.
- **Business Continuity**: If you own a business, life insurance can play a vital role in ensuring its continuity. It can provide funds for business partners or shareholders to buy out your share or cover any financial obligations tied to your role in the company.
- **Supplement Retirement Income**: Some life insurance policies, such as cash value or permanent life insurance, accumulate a cash value over time. This cash value can be accessed during your lifetime, providing a source of supplemental income in retirement or serving as an emergency fund.
- **Charitable Giving**: Life insurance allows you to leave a charitable legacy by naming a charitable organization as the beneficiary of your policy.
- **Peace of Mind**: Knowing that you have life insurance coverage can provide peace of mind. It offers reassurance that your loved ones will be financially protected and can maintain their standard of living if something were to happen to you.

Traditional Life Insurance	Living Benefits Life Insurance
☑ Death Benefit	☑ Death Benefit
	☑ Terminal Illness
	☑ Chronic Illness
	☑ Critical Illness
	☑ Medical Bills
	☑ Replacement Income

Get your mind on LIVING BENEFITS!

I encourage clients to purchase life insurance that has living benefits. Living Benefits Life Insurance allows you to **accelerate death benefits** if you get diagnosed with a terminal, critical or chronic illness or suffer a critical injury. Let's face it; most people get sick before they die. In 2018, **cancer patients paid $5.6 billion for out-of-pocket costs**. Not only did these patients have to pay these outrageous bills, but they missed work. With a living benefits policy, clients can accelerate up to 90% of their death benefits.

The accelerated benefit is tax-free, and you can use the money for whatever you need. A living benefits life insurance policy protects your savings, mortgage, and business. Many homeowners and small business owners are **one critical injury or illness away from bankruptcy**.

SCAN ME

Exercise: Scan the QR code to watch the video. Then list how many people you know who have or have had a critical illness (like cancer, stroke, heart attack), critical injury (like brain injury or paralysis), or chronic illness where they need help to bathe, eat, dress, go to toilet, or get out of bed. Did they need help financially?

Get your mind on THE BEST KEPT SECRET!

Yes, purchasing life insurance is to protect you and your family from financial devastation due to illness, injury, and death, but an insurance policy is also a **great wealth-building tool**. Every portfolio should include at least one insurance policy that is accumulating wealth. Money in an insurance policy accumulates and disbursed tax-free. And in most states, the cash value in an insurance policy is exempt from creditors.

The best-selling point of an Indexed Universal Life (IUL) insurance policy lies in its unique combination of life insurance protection and the potential for cash value growth tied to the performance of market indexes. Here are some key selling points of IUL policies:

Market Participation with Downside Protection: IUL policies offer the opportunity to earn interest or credited returns based on the performance of a specific market index, such as the S&P 500. This allows policyholders to participate in market gains without directly investing in the market. Importantly, IUL policies come with a downside protection feature, so even if the market index performs poorly, the policy's **cash value is never lost**.

Tax-Advantaged Growth: The cash value within an IUL policy **grows tax free.** You don't have to pay taxes on the gains as long as they remain within the policy. This tax advantage can enhance the growth potential of the cash value over time, allowing it to compound more efficiently.

Access to Cash Value: IUL policies allow policyholders to **access the accumulated cash value tax free through policy loans**. This can provide a source of funds for various purposes, such as emergencies, education expenses, or supplementing retirement income.

Legacy and Wealth Transfer: IUL policies can be an effective tool for transferring wealth to future generations. The death benefit paid to beneficiaries is **tax free income** and can provide a significant financial legacy.

Supplemental Retirement Income: The cash value growth within an IUL policy can serve as a source of supplemental income in retirement. By utilizing policy loans, policyholders can access the accumulated cash value to **supplement their retirement funds tax free**.

SCAN ME

Exercise: Scan the QR code to watch a video explaining the IUL. Learn more about indexed universal life insurance policies. There are some people who love them, but there are others who hate them. Decide for yourself by creating Pros and Cons lists.

Pros	Cons

Infinite Banking

You may have heard the term Infinite Banking because it is popular right now. Infinite banking is a financial concept that involves using a specially designed life insurance policy as a tool for personal banking and wealth accumulation. It allows individuals to take control of their finances and build a financial system that promotes growth, flexibility, and security.

Here's a simplified explanation of how infinite banking works:

01 **Life Insurance Policy: Infinite banking starts with the purchase of a participating whole life insurance policy or IUL. This policy combines a death benefit with a cash value component that grows over time. The policyholder pays regular premiums into the policy.**

02 **Tax Free Cash Value Accumulation: As the policyholder pays premiums, a portion of that money goes towards the cost of insurance, while the rest is invested in the cash value account. The cash value grows tax free.**

03 **Access Cash Value Tax Free : Over time, the cash value in the policy accumulates and becomes accessible to the policyholder tax free through policy loans. These loans are not the same as traditional loans from a bank. Instead, the policyholder is borrowing against the cash value they have built up. The policy itself acts as collateral, and the policyholder can use the loaned funds for any purpose, like buying real estate. These loans do not have to be paid back, but can be deducted from the death benefit.**

SCAN ME

Exercise: Scan the QR code to watch a free Infinite Banking workshop and take notes.

IT'S TIME TO ACT!

Your financial future is a significant consideration. Money can't buy happiness, but it does buy you the necessities to live a comfortable life. Financial mistakes can hold you back from living the life you deserve. **If you lack a financial plan for the future, then make one today.** If you're living outside your means, it's time to assess your spending and cut out unnecessary expenses. **Create a spending plan, and direct your money to your financial priorities.** Nobody wants to endure an emergency. However, you should expect the unexpected. Set up an emergency fund and be ready with the money needed to handle a crisis. Start saving for retirement right now! You will work hard for many years; retirement is your time to enjoy. Set your children up for financial success with a Millionaire Baby Plan. Last, purchase a sufficient amount of living benefits life insurance coverage for you and your entire family to protect your finances.

Be intentional with your money to reach financial freedom!

Here are ten steps you can take to be intentional about cultivating a healthy money mindset and creating generational wealth.

- **Set Clear Financial Goals**: Define your financial goals and create a roadmap to achieve them. Set specific, measurable, achievable, relevant, and time-bound (SMART) goals that align with your aspirations.
- **Think Long-Term**: Shift your mindset from short-term thinking to long-term thinking. Understand that building wealth takes time and consistent effort.
- **Embrace a Growth Mindset**: Adopt a mindset that sees failures and setbacks as opportunities for learning and growth. Embrace challenges and seek to expand your knowledge, skills, and abilities. Be open to new ideas and constantly look for ways to improve yourself and your financial situation.
- **Educate Yourself**: Make a commitment to continuous learning about personal finance, investing, and wealth-building strategies. Read books, attend seminars, listen to podcasts, and follow reputable financial experts who can provide valuable insights and guidance.
- **Surround Yourself with Like-Minded Individuals**: Surround yourself with people who have a positive and success-oriented mindset. Seek mentors, join mastermind groups, or engage in communities where you can learn from and be inspired by individuals who have achieved financial success.

- **Develop Financial Discipline**: Delay instant gratification and prioritize long-term financial goals over short-term desires. Develop the discipline to make wise financial choices and stick to them, even when faced with temptations.
- **Take Calculated Risks**: Building wealth often involves taking calculated risks. Be willing to step out of your comfort zone and seize opportunities that have the potential for high returns.
- **Maintain a Positive Money Mindset**: Cultivate a positive relationship with money. Avoid negative beliefs or attitudes that can hold you back from financial success.
- **Be Persistent**: Understand that building wealth is a journey that may involve obstacles and setbacks along the way. Develop persistence, resilience, and the ability to bounce back from failures. Learn from setbacks, make adjustments, and keep moving forward with determination.
- **Be Generous**: Develop a mindset of giving back and sharing your wealth. By helping others and contributing to causes you care about, you reinforce the abundance mindset and create a positive impact in the world. **

Creating wealth and a healthy money mindset is a gradual process that requires consistent effort, learning, and perseverance. It's important to **stay focused**, remain **adaptable** to changing circumstances, and stay **committed** to your long-term financial goals.

Blessings on your journey to financial freedom! Schedule a free Living Benefits Consult, Retirement Readiness Assessment, Be Your Own Bank Consult, or Millionaire Baby Consult with me to find out how I can help you plan, pocket, and protect your money at www.raykeltolson.com. (Scan barcode)

> “
>
> *"Summing it all up, friends, I'd say you'll do best by filling your minds and meditating on things true, noble, reputable, authentic, compelling, gracious—the best, not the worst; the beautiful, not the ugly; things to praise, not things to curse. Put into practice what you learned from me, what you heard and saw and realized. Do that, and God, who makes everything work together, will work you into his most excellent harmonies." -Philippians 4:8-9 (MSG)*

Dr. Raykel Tolson is a Financial Educator and the author of "Why Are Church Folk Poor." She inspires the children of God to elevate their financial mindset while providing practical solutions for growing and protecting their wealth. Dr. Tolson blends her extensive knowledge with a passion for teaching, equipping her clients with essential tools and strategies to transform their financial outlook. Through her books, workshops, and one-on-one coaching, Dr. Tolson offers clear, actionable steps to cultivate a mindset of abundance and proactive financial habits.

SCAN ME

Other Books by Raykel Tolson

Inspirational Non-Fiction

In "Why Are Church Folk Poor," the author explores a critical question: Why haven't many churchgoers embraced the prosperity that the law of attraction brings, despite its alignment with Biblical teachings? While the world has discovered the "Secret" and begun to thrive, many in the church remain hesitant to accept that this principle is indeed grounded in God's laws.

This easy-to-read reference book encourages readers to examine their relationship with money through the lens of scripture. The author skillfully blends Biblical verses with pop culture references to challenge and debunk common misconceptions about wealth. Each chapter concludes with exercises designed for self-analysis, helping readers to reflect and realign their financial beliefs.

"Why Are Church Folk Poor" is a must-read for Christians who are ready to embrace the abundant life that Jesus promised. It's a transformative guide for those looking to bridge the gap between their faith and their financial well-being.

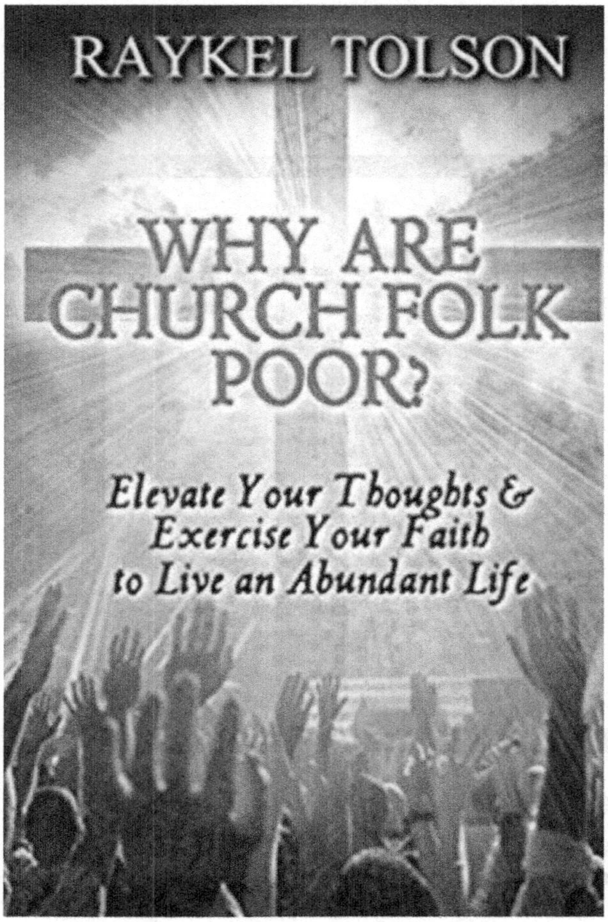

SCAN ME

Children's Picture Books

Co-authored with her son, Larenz Tolson, "Renz Bedtime Prayer" and "Renz Affirmations: God is Good and So Am I" are crafted to nurture resilience in young hearts. These books aim to strengthen children's relationship with God while helping them understand their inherent goodness and worthiness.

"Renz Bedtime Prayer" offers a soothing nightly routine that instills gratitude and peace.

"Renz Affirmations" empowers children with positive self-beliefs through uplifting affirmations.

SCAN ME

Inspirational Romances

Undefiled

A thought-provoking romance novella that seamlessly weaves themes of forgiveness, acceptance, love, and intimacy.

Liz and Anthony are thrown together when his mother falls ill. Attraction is instant, and love blooms quickly, but their happily-ever-after is threatened when Liz learns the truth about Anthony's sexuality the night before their wedding. Will she leave him at the altar?

SCAN ME

Christmas Novellas

Kelly Benson has spent the last five years hiding in Chicago after her crush, Gabe, brought a pregnant wife home to Shiloh. She moved to Chicago with hopes of landing her dream job but ended up settling for a job that merely pays the bills. Depressed and hopeless after being fired a week before Christmas, Kelly wishes for a Christmas Angel to come to work its magic.

SCAN ME

Holiday Love delves into the challenges and joys of a love that defies societal norms. It celebrates stepping out of comfort zones, the resilience of the human heart, and the beauty of taking a second chance love.

Made in the USA
Monee, IL
08 November 2026

67816233R00057